HISTORY ENCYCLOPEDIA

WORLD WAR II

An imprint of Om Books International

Contents

WORLD WAR II

1939–1945

The twentieth century witnessed two world wars. The First World War (World War I) was fought from 1914 to 1918. The Second World War (World War II) was fought from 1939 to 1945 and was fought in different parts of Europe, Russia, North Africa and Asia.

World War II had disastrous consequences and was called the deadliest war in human history, as 40 to 50 million people died.

World War II started in Europe, but spread throughout the world. It was fought between the Axis Powers comprising Germany, Italy, Japan and the Allied Powers comprising Britain, the USA, Soviet Union and France. Many other countries were also involved.

Much of the fighting occurred in Europe and in Southeast Asia (Pacific). The war ended with Germany's surrender on 7th May, 1945 while the war in the Pacific ended when Japan surrendered in September, 1945.

Invasion of France

Biplanes with airborne infantry.

Germany set its sights also on France. By 1940, German bombers had targeted air bases in France, Luxembourg, Belgium and the Netherlands and had destroyed many Allied planes. German paratroopers had also dented France's defence plans.

The Netherlands is invaded

German troops moved through Netherlands, northern Belgium, Luxembourg and into the Ardennes forest towards France. Oblivious to Germany's move to the south, the British and French army were stationed in large numbers in Belgium. However, Dutch resistance slowed down the advance of the German troops into Brussels and The Hague, but the German air force (Luftwaffe) bombed Rotterdam, just as surrender negotiations with the Netherlands were going on. The Rotterdam attack killed over 800 civilians, leading to the surrender of Netherlands.

German bunker in Normandy from World War II.

Belgium is invaded

Britain and France's plan to defend Belgium went awry because the German paratrooper units captured the forts between the cities of Antwerp and Liege on the first night of the invasion. Soon, the German forces attacked the Allied forces from the Ardennes forest in the south. Trapped between two determined German forces, the Allied forces could not stop the German advance towards Paris and the English Channel.

Attack on a German radar. Troops of the covering force and paratroopers practise withdrawal to the landing craft.

The Allied forces tried to battle it out with the 136 German divisions that entered Holland and Belgium. Simultaneously, around 2500 German aircrafts proceeded to bomb airfields in places across Belgium, Holland, France and Luxembourg. This was followed with 16,000 German airborne troops parachuting into Rotterdam, Leiden and The Hague. The Belgian bridges were soon captured by 100 German troops that came via air gliders. The Dutch army were outnumbered and defeated in five days. The day after, Belgium was invaded when the soldiers at Fort Eben-Emael surrendered.

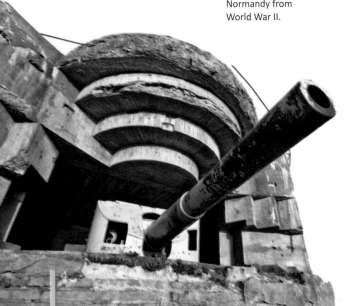

Evacuation from Dunkirk

Even as the French forces remained trapped between the two German troops, the British Expeditionary Force (BEF) was pushed back towards the French port of Dunkirk. With no hope of reaching the French forces, the English government ordered the BEF to retreat. Known as Operation Dynamo, the evacuation started on 27th May, 1940. Over seven days more than 800 civilian and military sea vessels were used to bring back close to 338,000 men to England. This evacuation meant that France was left to fight its own battle with Germany.

Ship leaving Dunkirk carrying defeated British and French soldiers to England. In the background the French port of Dunkirk burns under German advance.

France invaded

German tanks broke through the main fronts along the Somme River and the fortified Maginot Line, and entered Paris. To provide support, British Prime Minister Winston Churchill flew to Paris to offer his personal encouragement, but he could not spare any British military assistance because he needed them for England's defence. Italy opportunistically supported Germany and within four days the French capital fell and the French officials fled to Bordeaux. The French surrendered on 25th June, merely seven weeks after the invasion of France. Britain's forces at the Maginot Line surrendered at St Valéry as Prime Minister Churchill was reluctant to take any risk. On 22nd June, 1940, France signed an armistice with Germany. Hitler insisted that the armistice be signed in the same railway car that Germany had surrendered to France in 1918, at the end of World War I.

Leader of the National Socialists; and later Imperial Chancellor – Adolf Hitler.

Statue of Winston Churchill outside the Petit Palais near the Seine river.

FAST FACT

Winston Churchill had served as Britain's Prime Minister for only 16 days when the evacuation started.

Military evacuation of Dunkirk during World War II. Thousands of British and French troops wait on the dunes of Dunkirk beach for transport to England.

Italy Enters World War II

The Italian Government introduced military conscription in 1907. However, only about 25 per cent of those eligible for conscription received training and by 1912 there were only 300,000 men in the Italian Army. Over 5.2 million men served in the Italian Army during the First World War. Italy's total wartime casualties was 420,000 killed and almost 955,000 wounded.

Mussolini's statue on display at Militalia.

Signing of the Pact of Steel on 22nd May, 1939 in Berlin.

Benito Mussolini comes to power

Post World War I, Vittorio Orlando, the Italian representative at the Paris Peace Conference (1919) was criticised for changing Italy's stand. Benito Mussolini engineered the entry of Italian right-wing groups into the Fascist Party.

In 1920, the next Prime Minister Francesco Saverio Nitti was forced to resign and a series of riots beset Italy. Orlando also came under attack and was forced to resign in 1920. In 1922, King Victor Emmanuel III appointed Benito Mussolini in order to stop a communist revolution and consequently Mussolini became the head of a coalition comprising fascists and nationalists.

The Italian parliament continued to function for a while, but the murder of socialist leader Giacomo Matteotti in 1924 by the Fascists changed the face of Italy. Soon, communist or left-wing parties were censored. By 1929, Italy had become a one-party state.

Hitler and Mussolini in Munich, Germany on 18th June, 1940. Hitler was at a high point, as his army had accomplished a string of victories and was completing its conquest of continental Western Europe.

Pact of Steel

Hitler had for long been inspired by Mussolini's achievements. When Hitler came to power he wanted to develop a close relationship with the Italian dictator and secure for Germany another partner to fight against the Allies.

In 1936, Hitler secured Mussolini's partnership, after which the two leaders of Germany and Italy signed a military alliance thus, forming the Berlin-Rome Axis. By 1939, post the Italian invasion of Albania, Benito Mussolini signed a complete defence alliance with Germany, known as the Pact of Steel.

Liberty Ship SS Rowan explodes after being hit by a German bomb, near Sicily on 11th July, 1943.

FAST FACT

Benito Mussolini, the supreme dictator of Italy, believed in the concept of a fascist government, which has only one leader and one party that has complete power. The fascist government controls all the aspects of the lives of citizens..

Mussolini Plans to Invade Ethiopia

The African countries of Eritrea and Somalia were under Italy, but Ethiopia had managed to evade Italy's influence. Benito Mussolini was keen to occupy Ethiopia. In October 1935, Mussolini sent the Italian army under General Badoglio to Ethiopia. The League of Nations condemned Italy's move and imposed sanctions on Italy. Around 400,000 Italian troops fought with the poorly armed Ethiopian army and soon captured the capital Addis Ababa. In May 1936, Emperor Haile Selassie fled to England.

Mussolini and Hitler in Berlin.

Italian invasion of Ethiopia

Italy had previously tried to capture Ethiopia in 1896. But the Ethiopian forces had defeated Italy in the Battle of Adowa. A border skirmish between Ethiopia and Italian Somaliland in December 1934, gave Mussolini an excuse to invade Ethiopia. After Ethiopia's capture, Mussolini declared Italy's king Victor Emmanuel III emperor of Ethiopia and appointed Badoglio as viceroy.

Hitler and Mussolini join hands

Mussolini had always been an inspiration for Adolf Hitler. Hitler wanted a close relationship with Italy. Hitler extended an invitation to Mussolini to visit Germany. Post his visit, they signed a secret pact that promised Germany of Italian collaboration on certain diplomatic issues. When Mussolini visited Germany he saw many mass parades, military exercises and did a tour of the Krupp munitions factory. He left Germany as an altered individual who had new-found respect for the German dictator.

Hitler visits Mussolini

Similarly, when Hitler visited Mussolini's banquet, the German dictator promised that he would never break his Italian counterpart's trust and would never invade the Italian border.

In 1936, the two dictators joined hands in a military alliance. Italy entered World War II on Germany's side in 1940; thereby, declaring war on the Allies.

Statue of Haile Selassie.

FAST FACT

In 1919, Mussolini started the Fascist Party. He wanted to bring back the days of the Roman Empire. The members of the Fascist party wore black clothes known as "Black Shirts".

Stamp showing Benito Mussolini and Adolf Hitler 1941.

Adolf Hitler and Benito Mussolini being given a military salute during Hitler's visit to Venice, Italy.

Hitler Plans to Invade Britain

V1 flying bomb used by the Germans to attack London, England.

In 1940 Hitler issued Directive 16, that authorised the preparations to invade Britain. Hitler called the planned invasion as Operation Sea Lion. However, in reality, the operation was never carried out because Germany's plans went awry and they were ousted in the Battle of Britain.

Directive 16

Six weeks after Germany's invasion of France, the French signed an armistice with Germany. Britain remained the only country that continued to resist Germany's dominance. Hitler assumed that after France's surrender, the British would follow suit and also surrender. Nonetheless, when Britain remained steadfast in their resistance against the Germans, then Hitler issued Directive Number 16, which authorised a detailed plan to invade Britain, under Operation Sea Lion. The directive stated that the objective of the operation was "to eliminate the English motherland as a base from which war against Germany can be continued, and, if this should become unavoidable, to occupy it to the full extent".

Firemen at work in a bomb-damaged street in London during the Battle of Britain.

Germany's plan

The German Directive 16 included a plan to land along the southern coast of England, that extends from Dorset to Kent. The plan was that the German navy would defeat the Royal Navy in the Mediterranean and North Sea. The Royal Air Force had to be defeated and only then the actual invasion could happen.

Germany plans an air attack

Germany had control over the North Sea and France, which meant that the entire coastline near France was under its control and they could use the *Luftwaffe* (German air force) to attack Britain.

London's Big Ben surrounded with barbed wire and soldiers on guard during World War II.

World War II German jet fighters.

FAST FACT

Luftwaffe is a German term for air force and it became the official name for the Nazi air force. Founded in 1930 and commanded by Hermann Goering, the *Luftwaffe* became one of the largest commanding air forces in Europe during World War II.

Finnish and Russian Face Off

The Finnish Army was trained to use their terrain to the utmost advantage and were well adapted to the forests and snow-covered regions of their land. Finnish ski troops despite being mobile and well trained were not trained in large-scale exercises.

Soldiers of Finnish Guard sharpshooter battalion during Battle of Gorni Dubnik (Russo-Turkish War 1877-78).

A Finnish ski patrol, lying in the snow on the outskirts of Northern Finland, waiting for Russian troops on 12th January, 1940.

Winter war

Russia used 45 divisions with each division having 18,000 men (which in effect meant close to 25 per cent of Finland's population) and deployed 1500 tanks and 3000 planes. Finland did not have enough ammunition to fight the war. Russia was unequipped to handle a winter war and the winter of 1939-1940 was particularly severe.

Signing of the Moscow Peace Treaty

The Russians fought near the Russian–Finnish border and some parts of the 965 km border were utterly impassable. The Russian air force was also used only for a short while owing to the winter. The Russians saw heavy casualties and lost 800 planes. However, after renewed and reorganised military tactics, Russia managed to overcome the Finnish troops at the border. Finland agreed to give more territory to Russia and the Moscow Peace Treaty was signed.

Details about the treaty

As per the treaty, Finland ceded most of Finnish Karelia to Russia. The army and Finnish civilians were evacuated to the other side of the new border. The treaty also allowed free passage to Soviet civilians to Petsamo to move towards Norway. Under the treaty, Finland also ceded part of the Salla municipality and the islands near the Gulf of Finland. Further, as per the treaty Finland had to rent out the Hanko Peninsula for 30 years to the Soviets, who would proceed to use it as a naval base.

FAST FACT

Finland gave around 11 per cent of land and Russia got Lake Ladoga, giving Russia the safeguard that was required to protect Leningrad.

Old Russian tank used during World War II.

Italy Declares War Against Britain

A rusted helmet and machine-gun tape.

Dictator Benito Mussolini declared war on Great Britain and France and entered World War II. Mussolini's desire to expand Italy's empire to the Mediterranean and North Africa, made the dictator take this step, even if it meant going against the Italian monarch, King Vittorio Emmanuel III's wishes. The King mistrusted Germany, but his wishes went largely unnoticed and unheeded by Mussolini.

Mussolini's reasons for declaring war

Mussolini was upset with the sanctions placed by the League of Nations after its war with Ethiopia. Particularly since, the two countries that imposed sanctions, France and Britain, were themselves ruling over the rest of Africa. This pushed Mussolini towards agreeing to a pact with Hitler.

Allies push Italy to a war

The Allies ignored Italy's offer to declare a ceasefire when Germany invaded Poland. Soon, the Allies realised that Italy would get involved in the war and they started seizing German coal shipments that were making way to Italy. Italy was further humiliated and Mussolini condemned the Allies for this act and called it as piracy, since it was done to a state that was not at war with France and Britain.

The League of Nations condemned Italy's aggression and imposed sanctions, which included a ban on countries to sell arms, rubber and metals to Italy. There was opposition to the sanctions by some political leaders from France and Britain who thought that it would push Mussolini to form an alliance with Germany. In 1939, Italy invaded Albania and Mussolini signed a treaty to form an alliance with Hitler.

German soldiers during World War II.

The town of Cassino was completely destroyed in one of World War II's worst air bombings. The Monte Cassino Abbey was bombed in the same operation on 15th February, 1944.

Turmoil within Italy

Mussolini had comprehended that while peace would be more beneficial for Italy and a long drawn war could prove problematic for the country, he feared that if he did not join the war then he may not reap any benefits from it if the war was won by Germany—who would receive all the fruits of war.

Italy had begun to think that war was inevitable and the defeat of France and Britain seemed like a foregone conclusion, and Mussolini had a desire to dissolve the Italian monarchy. In fact, Italian Royalist members like Balbo, De Bono and De Vecchi asked King Emmanuel to revoke Mussolini's powers, but they did not make a strong push.

A British heavy gun in action, British soldiers preparing artillery shells and manning a large artillery piece.

Italy declares war on Britain

When Germany invaded Poland in 1939, Italy was not ready for a war, but Mussolini urgently wanted to join the war to be part of a historical event that could potentially change the map of Europe.

Italy had no great industrial prowess to brag about. In fact, it was not at all equipped like the countries of Britain, France or Germany as far as production of guns, ammunition, artillery, tanks, etc., was concerned.

Mussolini was perturbed at the shipping incident with the Allies. The Allies had not been overtly friendly towards Italy since World War I and the fact that now Italy's trade would also depend on the Allies was too much for Mussolini to handle. In 1940, he declared war on Britain.

Italy took part in the Battle of Britain along with Germany in 1940. Mussolini sent around 200 aircrafts to bomb Britain. However, the Italians achieved limited success due to the inferior quality of the Italian aircrafts.

They carried only 1,500 pounds of bombs per aircraft and conducted raids only during the nights or occasionally during the day.

Early 1900s World War II postcard depicting soldiers receiving machine gun instructions.

Machine gun Instructions - Camp Sherman,   Chillicothe, Ohio.

Kaiser Wilhelm II and König Victor Emanuel III und dem Kronprinzen Friedrich August von Sachsen bei der Herbstparade auf dem Tempelhofer Feld.

Kaiser Wilhelm II and King Victor Emmanuel III.

1939: Italy invades Poland

1940: Battle of Britain begins

FAST FACT

Poison gas was first used during World War I to dismantle the trench warfare stalemate. During World War II, Japan (in China) and Italy (in Ethiopia) used chemical weapons.

Battle of Britain

World War II German bomber.

The Battle of Britain began on 10th July, 1940 and lasted for three months with Germany bombing England. The name Battle of Britain comes from UK Prime Minister Winston Churchill's speech where he had reportedly said, "The Battle of France is over. The Battle of Britain is about to begin".

German Heinkel 111 bomber over London. Below is the river Thames and Tower Bridge.

Beginning of the battle

By the summer of 1940, German and British air forces had started battling it out in the sky over Britain and that was when the deadliest bombing campaign began. The Battle of Britain was fought essentially in the skies, but it ended when Germany's *Luftwaffe* couldn't supersede the efforts of the Royal Air Force despite Germany's continued targetting of Britain's air bases and posts.

Defeating the Royal Air Force

German troops soon realised that the British Royal Air Force (RAF) was a difficult adversary and hence if Britain had to be conquered, the RAF had to be destroyed. So, the German troops concentrated on destroying airport runways and targetted radar systems and infrastructure. The RAF and British forces continued to battle it out with Germany; whereby, Hitler decided to change strategy and started bombing large cities, starting with London.

Britain puts up a good defence

German troops began to feel that they were very close to conquering England, but the RAF shot down many German planes. Although the German troops continued bombing London and other targets in Britain, the raids had

The first mass German air raid on London on 7th September, 1940. Tower Bridge stands out against a background of smoke of fire.

to slow down because the RAF were fighting on their homeland, and they also had the advantage of radar facilities. They could, therefore, defend their aircrafts well.

Detail of the Battle of Britain Monument on the Victoria Embankment, London.

The USA Supports Britain

Although USA and England had similar ideologies, many in the US questioned its involvement during World War I. So, as far as possible USA did not want to get involved in World War II.

The Neutrality Act and the USA

At the advent of World War II in Europe, US President Franklin Roosevelt understood that the war could prove to be a menace for US security, so he sought ways to help European states without getting directly involved. The Neutrality Act came

A 1942 World War II poster of Uncle Sam. He holds a US flag and points his finger as fighting troops, with airplan es flying overhead, advance from a cloud of smoke.

Chinese soldier guards a line of American P-40 fighter planes, 1942.

into existence when the law was passed by the US Congress and signed by President Franklin Delano Roosevelt in August, 1935. It was meant to keep America out of any European conflict by banning shipment of any war material to the belligerents and it forbade US citizens from travelling on these ships and if they did it would be at their own risk. During the 1940s, when France had been invaded and Britain seemed to be the only democracy left, the USA began to trade arms under the fourth Neutrality Act that allowed USA to trade arms with the Allies.

Lend-Lease Act

In March 1941, Theodore Roosevelt allowed the lending, leasing, selling or bartering of arms under the Lend-Lease Act, which permitted ammunition and food to be given or leased to any state that the President deemed vital to the defence of USA. The Lend-Lease Act of 1941 began a programme under which the USA could provide goods and services to the Allies in their war against Germany, Italy and later Japan during World War II. As per the terms under the Lend-Lease Act, the Allies could repay America by way of returning the goods or using them in support of the cause or by a similar transfer of goods.

Theodore Roosevelt, waving his hat, as he stands in car.

1935: The Neutrality Act passed

1941: The Lend-Lease Act passed

13

USA and Britain's Association

USA was pulled into World War II when its naval and air force began accompanying British convoys that were transporting the Lend-Lease material across the seas, in a bid to defend them from the German U-boats. Winston Churchill kept urging US President Theodore Roosevelt to enter the war. They met at the 1941 Atlantic Conference, where Roosevelt had said that people should have the right to choose their own government.

The USS Shaw on fire after being hit by a Japanese bomber in Pearl Harbor.

The final trigger

The 1941 Japanese bombing of the US Pacific fleet at Pearl Harbor became the final trigger that ensured the entry of USA into World War II. After the bombing, the US Senate unanimously voted in favour of entering the war, except for one congressman. Four days later, Germany declared war on USA.

USA enters World War II with Operation Torch

In November 1942, the combined armed forces of USA and Britain began an ambitious operation against the French-held territories in Algeria and Morocco. The campaign was called Torch. It was born out of several rounds of discussions and disagreements.

In 1942, Operation Torch or the invasion of North Africa became USA's first offensive during World War II. Allied troops steadily cornered German forces in North Africa and Germany surrendered in Tunisia in May, 1943. The Allied forces realised that Russia needed help. Churchill's plan of an attack through Italy at the Casablanca conference was approved and Operation Husky or the invasion of Sicily began in July 1943. By June 1944, the Allied forces had captured Rome.

Operation Torch plaque.

Eight US Navy Douglas SBD-3 Dauntless dive bombers and six Gruman F4F-4 Wildcat fighters on the flight deck of the escort carrier USS Santee (ACV-29) during Operation Torch, the November 1942 invasion of North Africa.

Operation Barbarossa

Operation Barbarossa: Germans inspecting Russian planes.

The operation by Germany to invade Russia on 22nd June, 1941 was code-named Operation Barbarossa. It became the largest military attack during World War II and had lasting effects on the people of Russia. Around three million Axis troops and 3500 tanks were part of this operation. Germany's win against the Allies in France a year earlier was a trigger for the operation.

The Soviet surviving

Germany in its triumph was happy to note that the Soviet army had previously faced defeats at the hands of Finland in 1939. This operation became one of the crucial moments of World War II. Unlike what Germany had in mind, the Soviet forces fought and survived, and ensured that the German offensive was thwarted.

Blitzkrieg and Operation Barbarossa

Operation Barbarossa was based on the idea of a huge attack that follows the blitzkrieg method—blitzkrieg is the German word for lightning war—it was a military tactic that was designed to create a huge disruption within enemy lines through the use of mobile forces and fire arms. Three German army groups attacked Russia on 22nd June, 1941.

German soldiers at Lubnica, where Soviet (Russian) forces attacked their left flank in 1941.

Marcks plans attack on Russia

Erick Marcks, the German General, came up with an initial plan that involved a huge attack on Moscow followed by a second attack on Kiev with two

Destroyed Soviet tanks at Junourcia, during the German invasion of the USSR (Russia) in 1941.

subsequent attacks in the Baltic near Leningrad and in Moldavia in the south. After Moscow's decline, Marcks planned another attack on Kiev. Marcks' plan was reworked by Halder, but the final change was made by Hitler who code-named it Barbarossa.

FAST FACT

Hitler had outlined his desire to invade the Soviet Union in his 1925 book *Mein Kampf*. Operation Barbarossa was a culmination of this desire.

Hitler's Plan

As per Hitler's plan, the main military action would happen in the north, which meant that Leningrad would become an equally important target along with Moscow. The attack involved the combined military strength of the Axis powers – three million soldiers, 3580 tanks, 7184 artillery guns, 1830 planes and 750,000 horses. On the seventeenth day of Operation Barbarossa, 300,000 Russians were captured. More than 2500 Russian tanks, 1400 Russian artillery guns and 250 Russian aircrafts were captured.

Nazi anti-Semitic poster of the early 1940s.

Russia is devastated

The German troops advanced very quickly and took over the Russian army's supply and communication lines. Hitler ordered his troops to move southeast towards Kiev. Another set of troops was asked to move to the north. This diversion meant that his central troops were left exposed without two of its most powerful groups.

Major success in Russia

The German troops saw many successes in the north and south. Many Russian soldiers were captured and held as prisoners. The German troops also amassed huge quantities of Russian arms and ammunition. The unprepared Soviet forces were taken aback with the sudden blitzkrieg attacks from Germany along the long border that stretched for close to 2900 km. The Soviet forces had to face terrible losses and in a week's time the German army had advanced 322 km into Soviet territory. The Germans had destroyed close to 4000 aircrafts and had either killed, captured or injured close to 600,000 Red Army troops. However, the diversion also impacted the time that the German troops took to advance further. Further, the German Army was caught in the midst of terrible cold and the freezing temperatures, which also affected their advance.

German infantry advancing on a burning village in Russia.

A Soviet military SSh-40 helmet emblazoned with the red star.

FAST FACT

Blitzkrieg is a German word, which means lightning war. It refers to a military tactic involving a quick, sudden and overwhelming attack on the enemy.

1939: German-Soviet Pact signed

1941: Operation Barbarossa begins

German anti-tank gun team on road with a flaming tank in background in Russia.

Invasion of USSR

Germany along with the Axis powers invaded the Soviet Union under Operation Barbarossa on 22nd June, 1941. It was one of Germany's biggest military operations during World War II. Around 4.5 million troops attacked from Polish territory that was under Germany's control. Despite the non-aggression pact signed in 1939, both the countries had been expecting aggression from the other side, but both were only waiting for the right time to strike.

First day of the German Invasion of the Soviet Union in June 1941.

Beginning of the Russian invasion

Hitler had always wanted to remove the communist threat from Russia and had, therefore, seen the 1939 German-Soviet nonaggression pact with Russia as just a temporary arrangement. After the German invasion of France and the other Low countries (Belgium, the Netherlands and Luxembourg), Hitler signed Directive 21, which gave the first operational order for the invasion of the Soviet Union under Operation Barbarossa.

Reenactment of breaking the siege of Leningrad.

Two years after signing the German–Soviet Pact, Germany made a move to invade Russia. The German troops saw success in Minsk and Smolensk and soon reached Kiev.

During the winter and autumn of 1941, special units of German Security Police and Service were deployed at the front lines.

Severity of winter

The winter of December 1941 proved to be very harsh for the German armed forces as they marched their way to Moscow.

The winter gave Russia that much needed break from a continuous battle with Germany, but there were huge losses from both sides.

Order of German Cross in gold.

Russian soldiers burned to death during the German invasion of the Soviet Union in 1941.

Failure of Barbarossa

Red Army section in Olšanské cemetery.

Hitler's strategy relied heavily on the internal collapse of the Red Army. But that was not how things panned out. The Germans had not anticipated the harsh winter and difficult terrain of Russia, which would make managing its army difficult. The Russian army was initially debilitated. However, soon it reorganised and its counterattacks soon forced the weary and resource-deficit German army to accept defeat.

Difficulty in coordination

Hitler deployed his armed forces to different places – Leningrad, Moscow and present day Ukraine. During the first six weeks Russia fought back, but soon German forces reached Leningrad and invaded Smolensk and Dnepropetrovsk in Ukraine.

However, coordinating with various army groups spread over a million kilometres proved to be very cumbersome and it was something that Hitler had not counted upon.

Unforeseen obstacles

The German troops trudged towards Moscow during the severe winter and were slowed down by Russia's counterattacks, forcing the Germans to retreat. The German soldiers were tired; they had ill-planned their warfare and could not provide for food and medicines. The distances were too large and the end goal was huge. The German armed forces also had to deal with poor Russian roads and harsh weather. Further, the Germans underestimated the resistance that they would face from the Red Army.

The German Falke Division crossing the Bug River, while advancing towards Kiev in September 1941.

German troops reach Stalingrad

Russia managed to drive the Germans back from Moscow. However, after a short while the German troops regrouped and continued their offensive in the city of Stalingrad, moving towards the Caucasus oil fields.

Operation Barbarossa became one of the most crucial events during World War II. Despite suffering huge losses, Russia bravely fought and continued to fight the Germans until 1942.

Russian soldiers preparing to cross a river in Stalingrad during the Battle of Stalingrad.

War in China

In 1941, Japan attacked Pearl Harbor thus, forcing the US to join World War II. The attack and the simultaneously occurring second Sino-Japanese war led to Japan making many enemies. In 1933, Japan left the League of Nations and became a threat for the European powers and USA. At the start of the second Sino-Japanese war, USA imposed economic sanctions on Japan.

Digital oil painting of an attack during World War II.

Japan vs China

The second Sino-Japanese war began in July 1937 when the Japanese fired at Chinese troops at the Marco Polo Bridge near Beijing as an excuse to launch an invasion on China, using Manchuria as their base.

Soon, China's most important port, Shanghai was conquered and later the capital Nanjing (Nanking) was captured in December 1937. Following this, in 1940, Japan joined the Axis powers and signed the Tripartite Pact along with Germany.

In 1941, the Chinese Nationalists fought with the Japanese forces under the leadership of Chiang Kai-Shek. Chiang's forces were not well trained and were unequipped. World War II had reduced the foreign aid that China used to receive.

In 1942, the US Congress approved a US$ 500 million loan for China as USA saw China as its main ally against Japan.

End of the Sino-Japanese war

There were delays in supplies reaching China and it did not help that Chiang and his allies could not reach a consensus on how to use the foreign aid. However, China kept resisting the Japanese attacks.

FAST FACT

The second Sino-Japanese War (1937-1945), fought between China and Japan, was the largest war in Asia of the twentieth century.

Chinese soldiers marching on the Burma Road toward the fighting line on the Salween river front in 1943.

By 1944, Japan had invaded Kiangsi and Kwangsi and later controlled Peking-Hankow railway.

However, the second Sino-Japanese war came to an end when the US dropped the world's first atomic bombs on the cities of Hiroshima and Nagasaki, Japan on 6th and 9th August, 1945. The bombings led to Japan's surrender.

Hiroshima bomb explosion on 6th August, 1945.

Fall of Mussolini

Benito Mussolini, the founder of fascism, was Italy's supreme leader and dictator from 1922 till 1943. He became an important ally of Germany and Japan during World War II. In May 1938, Mussolini decided to partner with Hitler during the war. However, his armed forces were not prepared for war and could, therefore, offer no resistance to the Allied forces. Even internally Mussolini faced resistance to his dictatorship, which resulted in him becoming unpopular in his own country. He was overthrown in 1943. The Italian insurgents who opposed him captured and murdered the former Italian dictator. Thus, Mussolini's reign ended.

Meeting of Adolf Hitler and Benito Mussolini in Stepina, 1941.

(From left) Emilio De Bono, Benito Mussolini, Italo Balbo and Cesare Maria De Vecchi during the march to Rome.

Benito becomes Italy's supreme leader

Mussolini was involved in socialist politics and was a journalist in the socialist press. He joined the Italian army in September 1915.

By 1919, he formed the Fascist Party and got support from unemployed war veterans. He armed these party members and they began to be called Black Shirts. Mussolini's Black Shirts terrorised political leaders and were finally asked by the Italian king to join the coalition government in 1921.

Mussolini forms a government

In 1922, Mussolini was asked by King Victor Emmanuel to form the government. He became the Prime Minister of Italy. Slowly and steadily, he dissolved the various democratic institutions in the government and silenced all his political opponents. By 1925, he declared himself as a dictator and took the title of "Il Duce".

He wanted to re-establish Italy as a great European power and with that intent he invaded Ethiopia in 1935. Mussolini helped the Spanish dictator Franco in the Spanish Civil war. He signed the Pact of Steel with Germany and introduced an anti-Jewish legislation in Italy.

Mussolini with Italian troops in the Adriatic front.

1919: Mussolini forms Fascist Party

1925: Mussolini takes title of 'Il Duce'

Mussolini Declares War on Allies

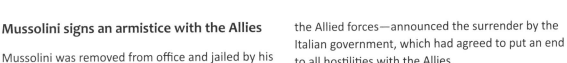

In 1940, Mussolini declared war on Britain and France, and met with a series of defeats in north and east Africa and the Balkans. By 1943, Italy was severely defeated and the Allied forces had captured Sicily.

Anzio War Cemetery for allied military personnel who were killed in World War II.

Mussolini signs an armistice with the Allies

Mussolini was removed from office and jailed by his ex-colleagues in the Fascist government. Italy signed an armistice with the Allies. The German troops came and rescued Mussolini. He was reinstated as the leader of the government, but in reality he did not have any influence.

Fall of Mussolini

Mussolini had dreamt of establishing a Fascist Italy and bringing it back to its former glory as an empire, but Italy suffered many military defeats during World War II. By 1943, opposition groups in Italy had come together to overthrow Mussolini and make peace with the Allies, but the Germany's army stopped such an act. However, after Italy lost its ground, Mussolini was soon deposed in a coup.

Announcement of surrender

After Italy signed an armistice with the Allies, General Eisenhower—the commander-in-chief of the Allied forces—announced the surrender by the Italian government, which had agreed to put an end to all hostilities with the Allies.

In a personal message to his people, Prime Minister Badoglio confirmed the surrender. It was suggested to sign an armistice in August in a neutral territory. Finally, the armistice was signed on 3rd September, 1943 in Sicily. They decided to keep the armistice a secret until the Allies had completed its invasion of Italy.

Benito Mussolini met with a series of defeats between 1940-43.

Bomb-struck area in Germany.

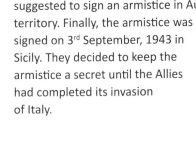

Russia Declares War on Japan

A World War II US fighter plane shooting down Japanese torpedo bomber over Saipan.

In the east, the Japanese army had been eyeing the Siberian part of Russia for a very long time and tried several times to challenge the Russian forces in the region. The two countries eventually signed a ceasefire and the two countries remained friendly right up to World War II. As per his agreement with the Allies, Stalin led Russia to declare war on Japan just three days after the Hiroshima atomic bomb attack, after which Russia invaded Manchuria.

Ruins of Nagasaki, Japan, after the atomic bombing of 9th August, 1945. Battered religious figures are seen amid the rubble.

Operation August Storm

In a surprise move for the Japanese, Russia declared war on Japan on 8th August, 1945 and launched Operation August Storm. After the destruction of Hiroshima, Japan still had ammunition and fought the Russians. Once the Russians invaded Manchuria, they defeated the Japanese army. Soon, the Soviet forces launched an attack on the south of Sakhalin Island, after which they planned to invade the island of Hokkaido. Japan understood that it would not be possible for its army to fight both the Allies and Soviet armed forces, both of which would be attacking its territory from different directions. The Soviet invasion decimated the Japanese armed forces. On 9th August, 1945 USA dropped another

atomic bomb on Nagasaki and by 15th August, 1945 Emperor Hirohito of Japan officially surrendered to the Allies.

Russia continues fighting with Japan

Russian forces continued fighting with the Japanese Kwantung Army. After two weeks, the Japanese forces lay defeated and Japan's official surrender to the Allies was quickly signed on 2nd September, 1945 on the US Battleship Missouri.

The Atomic Dome, ex Hiroshima Industrial Promotion Hall, destroyed by the first atomic bomb in Hiroshima, Japan.

Mushroom cloud of the atom bomb that exploded over Nagasaki, Japan, on 9th August, 1945.

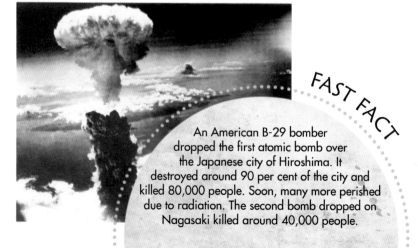

FAST FACT

An American B-29 bomber dropped the first atomic bomb over the Japanese city of Hiroshima. It destroyed around 90 per cent of the city and killed 80,000 people. Soon, many more perished due to radiation. The second bomb dropped on Nagasaki killed around 40,000 people.

Allies Invade Italy

The Allied invasion of Sicily became the reason for the fall of Mussolini's government. He was forced to resign by the Fascist Grand Council and was soon arrested. After the Italian dictator was deposed, Pietro Badoglio became the leader of the Italian government. He held secret negotiations with the Allies notwithstanding the presence of German troops in Italy.

US B-17 Bomber falling after its wing was shot off during invasion of Sicily in July 1943.

The Eighth Army

The Allied invasion of Italy was led by Field Marshal Bernard L. Montgomery, who along with the Allied troops crossed the Straits of Messina from Sicily and headed towards Calabria, also known as the "toe" of Italy. Montgomery's British Eighth Army began advancing through the Italian mainland. As per Italy's surrender terms, the Allies would be lenient with the Italians if they would help the Allies in defeating the German armed forces in Italy.

Italy's invasion begins

By 1943, the Allied forces had begun their invasion of European countries under the control of the Axis powers. It started with the island of Sicily as they faced very little struggle from the dispirited Italian troops. In just three days, around 150,000 Allied troops arrived on Italy's shore and soon the Allied invasion of Sicily was complete.

Secret negotiations with Allies

The collapse of Mussolini seemed imminent with the Allied conquest of Sicily. The Fascist Grand Council forced Mussolini to resign and he was soon arrested. Pietro Badoglio took over the reigns of the Italian government after secret negotiations with the Allies. Mussolini who was imprisoned in the Abruzzo mountains was rescued by German commandos and reinstated as a leader with very little power.

FAST FACT

Mussolini tried to escape from Italy, but was caught by Italian partisans and shot dead on 28th April, 1945.

World War II era bombing run on airport.

Operation Husky

The Allies wanted to challenge Germany by overthrowing the Italian regime. Further, invading Italy seemed like a good option because it would divert Germany's attention from the Allied plan of Germany's invasion. The Allies started the Italian campaign with Sicily's invasion. The Allies named the invasion of Sicily as Operation Husky.

World War II German bunker in Marina di Ragusa, Sicily, Italy.

Capture of Palermo

After defeating the German forces in the mountains of Sicily, the Allies successfully managed to send back the German forces. The capture of Palermo inevitably led to the collapse of Mussolini's government. In this attack, the Allies suffered casualties of over 23,000. The Allies decided on Operation Husky after they realised that the best way to tackle Germany would be by invading Sicily. General Dwight D. Eisenhower became the overall commander of the attack, while British General Harold Alexander became the overall ground commander. The invasion was done using gliders, parachutes and boats. Despite disruptions caused by the high winds, after a while the Sicilian capital of Palermo was conquered by the Allies and Sicily was secured.

German forces resist Allies in Italy

Despite the surrender of the Italian government, the German troops fought and resisted the fall of Rome. The German-fortified Winter Line across southern Italy kept pushing back the Allied forces for more than six months. Finally, in 1944, Rome was conquered and the German troops retreated towards a new line called the Gothic Line towards northern Italy, which they managed to control till 1945.

Allied ships in a southern Italian port being loaded with vehicles and supplies. They assaulted the southern coast of France, in Operation Dragoon on 15th August, 1944.

Mussolini is executed

The Badoglio government declared war on Germany and by April 1945 the Allied forces had started a new offensive. Mussolini was captured again and executed by Italian partisans.

A bronze statue of Dwight D. Eisenhower in his World War II jacket. The statue is on the grounds of the Presidential Library and Museum, USA.

Operation Husky's battle plan for the invasion of Sicily in the White House Map Room.

FAST FACT

During the invasion of Italy, the Allies suffered casualties of over 23,000, while the Axis powers had casualties of around 29,000 even as more than 130,000 soldiers were taken as prisoners of war.

A-20 G Havoc light bomber with D-Day "invasion stripes" painted on wings. Plumes of smoke rise from the Forest Cerisy, where a German machine gun position blocked the US advance, 8th June, 1944.

Allies Invade Western Europe

The battle of Normandy lasted from June to August 1944. It led to the freedom of western Europe from Germany's control. Called as Operation Overlord and also known as D-Day, the Battle of Normandy involved around 156,000 Allied forces comprising British, Canadian and American soldiers who landed along the coastline of Normandy in France. The Battle of Normandy ended with the Allies freeing various countries in western Europe from Germany's control.

FUN FACT

The Normandy American Cemetery near the Omaha beach and the English Channel was the first US cemetery in Europe. More than 9300 of the US armed forces who died during the D-Day Normandy missions were buried in the cemetery.

The coast of Normandy is covered with deep craters from the bombardments on D-day.

Normandy landing

The Normandy invasion saw US, British, and Canadian forces land on five beaches in Normandy. Later, other countries also joined them. The invasion led by 12 countries involved three million troops.

D-day

Launched on 6th June, 1944, the first day of the Normandy landing is also called D-day. The Allied troops crossed the English Channel to reach Normandy in France. It ended in the defeat of the Germans and the liberation of northern France.

1943 American poster showing cannons, each with the flag of an Allied nation.

Beginning of end of World War II

Owing to the fact that the Battle of Normandy was fought on land and in water, a lot of planning was required to conduct detailed overtures that would mislead the Germans. By August 1944, the operation had succeeded in liberating northern France and by the next spring the Allies had defeated the Germans. It is no wonder that the Battle of Normandy is also called the Beginning of the end of World War II, at least in Europe.

D-Day landing crafts head for Omaha beach during the Normandy invasion on 6th June, 1944. In the right is the cruiser USS Augusta, flagship of the Western Naval Task Force.

Operation Overlord

On 5th June, 1944, more than 5,000 ships carrying troops and supplies left England for France, even as over 11,000 aircrafts were being readied for air warfare to support the invasion of France. The invasion began on the morning of 6th June, 1944. Around 156,000 allied troops effectively invaded the beaches of Normandy. Within a week the beaches were fully secured.

Formation of Douglas A-20s over France during the D-Day invasion in June 1944.

Choltitz refuses Hitler

Paris finally became free after four years of Nazi occupation when the French 2nd Armoured Division and the US 4th Infantry Division were able to overcome the weakened German resistance. Hitler ordered the German army to bomb Paris's major landmarks and burn the city before the Allies reached and liberated the city. However, General Dietrich von Choltitz, the commander of the German garrison, did not pay heed to Hitler's orders and signed a formal surrender.

Germany deterred

Due to the absence of Commander Rommel (who was on leave), Hitler did not send divisions close to Normandy to counterattack the Allies. The German troops came from other places and were delayed as many bridges had been destroyed by the Allied forces. Soon, the port of Cherbourg was conquered and more Allied forces entered Normandy.

France liberated

By the end of August 1944, the Allied forces had liberated Paris and soon the German forces were pushed back. The Allied forces entered Germany. On the other side, Russian forces too had begun to advance into Germany. When Germany was unable to defeat the Allies in Normandy, it had to concede its failure in defending what it had wanted to create—"the European fortress". The loss of Normandy led to the end of World War II.

German bunker at Point du Hoc in Normandy, France.

1944: Operation Overlord begins

1945: Second World War ends

Mulberry harbour developed for the D-Day invasion of Normandy. Installed on Omaha beach after D-Day, the steel roadway was supported by prefabricated concrete caissons.

German Offensive in the West

The Battle of the Bulge started in December 1944 and earned its name owing to the bulging shape in the map. It became the last big offensive on the Western Front and was the biggest battle that the US fought. The battle was fought during the winter from 1944–1945 and was the final major German attack against the Allies in World War II.

American soldiers, stripped of equipment, lie dead, face down in Belgium during the Battle of the Bulge. The soldier in the foreground has bare feet.

Divide and rule

The Battle of the Bulge was Hitler's final attempt to split the Allied forces. It started on 16th December, 1944 and was carried out because Hitler believed that the Allied forces were weaker in western Europe. He believed that a major attack would completely destroy the Allies.

Battle of the Bulge

In a desperate attempt at regaining lost ground, the German army launched the attack against the Allies in the thickly forested Ardennes region in Belgium, which proved to be costly for the Allies.

The Battle of the Bulge got its name because the attack created a 113 km wide and 80 km deep bulge in the American defensive line thus, separating the British and American forces.

Germany faces shortage of fuel

Despite heavy casualties, the US army did not give up. Soon, the German forces faced a shortage of fuel, while the Allied troops led by General Patton regrouped and fought hard to retrieve the town of Bastogne in Belgium.

The main reason for the shortage of fuel was that the American troops had bombed and destroyed the German fuel depots, which led to the German tanks running out of fuel. The Germans lost the battle.

German soldier waving his unit members forward in the first few days of the Battle of the Bulge.

Russian old gun in Prokhorovka on 30th January, 2013. The largest tank battle of World War II happened here.

Valiant US Troops Don't Give Up

During the Battle of the Bulge, the American troops near Bastogne, Belgium were surrounded by the Germans army and they were ordered to surrender or die. But the US troops led by US General McAuliffe did not give up and held out till more reinforcement troops arrived. The courage of these valiant soldiers ensured the victory of the Allies in the battle.

Gestapo officials recording data on incoming prisoners at a German concentration camp.

Bodies of dead inmates in the yard of Nordhausen, a Gestapo concentration camp. The photo was taken shortly after the camp's liberation by the US Army on 12th April, 1945.

Germany surrenders

In April 1945, the commander of the German home guards (Gestapo), Heinrich Himmler, entered into negotiation talks for peace with the Allies, that is, Britain and USA. Meanwhile, rather than face arrest by the Allies, Adolf Hitler committed suicide in Berlin on 30th April, 1945. Soon, the Allies demanded that the German troops immediately surrender at all their fronts.

End of the European phase of war

In 1945, Colonel General Alfred Jodl became the German High Command. He was Hitler's successor.

In the beginning, General Jodl did not want the Germans to surrender at all the fronts, but wanted only the forces that were fighting in western Europe to surrender. However, the Allied commander General Dwight Eisenhower wanted a complete German surrender. Eisenhower gave the indication that if Germany failed to completely surrender, then the Allies would seal off the western front and not allow the Germans to escape to the west, which meant that they would ultimately fall in front of the approaching Soviet forces. On 7th May, 1945, early in the morning, Colonel General Alfred Jodl signed the terms of unconditional surrender and after five years, eight months and seven days, the European phase of World War II came to an end.

Germany surrender document signed by Gen. Alfred Jodl, Chief of Staff of the German Army. It was signed at the Allied Headquarters at Reims, on 7th May, 1945.

Allied POWs in a variety of uniforms at a prison camp in Zossen, Germany.

FUN FACT

The Gestapo was the political police of Nazi Germany, that ruthlessly eliminated opposition to the Nazis within Germany and its occupied territories. Working in partnership with the Sicherheitsdienst or the Security Service, it was primarily responsible for the roundup of Jews throughout Europe for deportation to extermination camps.

The German Collapse

The Allied forces extensively used air warfare in their final attack on Germany. The air offensive included 800 RAF aircrafts and 400 US aircrafts and resulted in the death of around 25,000 people and destruction of various cities across Europe.

Germans and the self-destruct mode

The German troops were asked to follow Hitler's idea of self-destruction. Hitler had declared that "the battle must carry on without consideration for our own population" and that all "all industrial plants, all the main electricity works, waterworks and gas works" must be destroyed to create a desert-like environment for the Allies. Hitler's self-destruct idea met with opposition from his Minister of War Production Albert Speer, who secretly met army and industrial heads and asked them not to heed Hitler's idea.

Allied forces enter Berlin

The Allied forces comprising mainly Americans and British soldiers crossed the Rhine river and easily reached Berlin. Simultaneously, Russia took the offensive towards Vienna and soon the Russians too reached Berlin.

Germany was bound to lose the war from the beginning

Germany's strategic position even at the start of the war had never been optimum, for it was at war with countries like France and UK that together had a population of around 90 million.

They were industrialised nations that received help from neutral countries like Belgium and the Netherlands—countries who were in essence enemies of Germany. Germany had a population of just 79 million.

Further, the French and British navies prevented Germany from accessing its natural resources. Thus, due to these factors Germany was bound to run out of the raw materials required to fight this prolonged battle.

Consequently, Germany was forced to surrender in the end.

Bodies of prisoners who died of starvation lie on the floor of a concentration camp in Nordhausen, Germany after liberation by First US Army on 11th April, 1945.

FUN FACT

The German air force had 22 infantry divisions, two armour divisions and 11 para-troop divisions. Further, 84 German army generals were executed by Hitler.

In May 1941, Nazi Germany bombed British cities.

Hitler with Baldur von Schirach, who was the leader of the "Hitler Youth".

Hitler Stays in Berlin

During the last 10 days of his life, Hitler met his top men and fellow Nazis. He met Josef Goebbels and Himmler, Ribbentrop and Alfred Jodl among others on his 56th birthday in Berlin. They asked him to leave the now doomed Berlin and go towards the mountainous terrain of the German–Austrian border, where he had his villa. They urged him to go there and could continue to hold the fort in the mountains of western Austria and southern Bavaria.

The fall of Hitler

Hitler knew that if he moved out of his bunker in Berlin he would risk being captured. He did not want to be alive and end up being caught and displayed by his enemies, especially the Russians. Therefore, he did not leave, but gave permission to his personal bunker staff to leave. A few of his personal staff stayed with him, including his top aide Martin Bormann, some soldiers, some of his private secretaries and his long-time companion, Eva Braun. Hitler chose to stay in Berlin and married his mistress Eva Braun two days before he committed suicide with her in the chancellery ruins. Around this time the Russian troops were just a few kilometres away from Hitler's complex.

Germany surrenders

Hitler's successor, Dönitz, wanted to save Germany's civilians and he worked towards this aim. The Allied forces finally broke through the German defences. The surrender document was signed on 29th April, 1945 and the attacks soon stopped by 2nd May, 1945.

Helmet and rifle monument to dead soldiers on a shell-blasted beach.

As infantrymen march through a German town, a shocked old woman stares at the ruins in Germany in 1945.

The European World War ends

The German forces surrendered and signed a surrender document at Montgomery's headquarters and another one at Reims in front of the American, British and French delegations. By midnight of 8th May, 1945 the war in Europe was formally over.

FUN FACT

The United Nations was formed at the end of World War II with an aim to prevent such wars in the future.

US Troops Continue Attacks on Japan

Towards the end of 1942, the Japanese soldiers had begun to occupy or attack different places across the South Pacific. Hoping to stop Japan in its tracks, the US Navy Admiral Chester Nimitz followed a strategy of island hopping, that is, to capture strategic islands near Japan one by one, so that eventually the US bombers would reach within closing distance of Japan.

Aerial view of Hitachi Aircraft Co., in Tachikawa, Japan. It was bombed by US B-29 Superfortresses in 1945.

USA uses firebombs

After securing the Japanese island of Iwo Jima, USA tried a new strategy of night strikes using napalm firebombs. The Tokyo bombing on 9th and 10th March, 1945 devastated the city and killed more than 80,000 people and rendered over a lakh Japanese homeless.

Aerial warfare against Japan

The American troops continued to bomb cities like Kobe, Yokohama, Toyama, Osaka and Nagoya. It seemed as if Japan did not require any invasion on land and that simple air warfare would suffice. The USA with its Manhattan Project under its US Office of Scientific Research and Development soon developed an atomic bomb that was tested in the desert area

near Alamogordo, New Mexico, in July 1945. The atomic bomb had the same potency as 15,000 tons of dynamite. President Truman saw the possibility of using the atomic bomb in Japan, particularly because Japan did not respond well to the Potsdam declaration. The Hiroshima bombing had a devastating effect. It killed more than 70,000 people and many more died due to radiation exposure. The second bombing on Nagasaki killed around 40,000 people. Finally, Japan's Emperor Hirohito surrendered to the Allies.

An Army B-25 bomber takes off from the USS HORNET in the first US air raid on Japan led by General James Doolittle on 18th April, 1942.

Costs of World War II

World War II became the most terrifying and significant event of the twentieth century. It was responsible for many social changes that ended European colonialism and brought forth the US civil rights movement. In addition, it may have paved way for the start of the women's rights movement.

Emergence of two superpowers

After World War II, two major powers emerged —USA and Soviet Russia. Soon, the two countries would delve into a war of another kind — the Cold War that would last for the remainder of the twentieth century.

Cost of World War II

World War II was the worst war in history and although the exact figure of human lives that were lost across the world is not known, it is estimated that more than 50 million defence personnel and civilians might have died during World War II. The countries that suffered the most in terms of losses, both human and material, included Japan, China, Germany and Russia.

Loss of life

Estimates suggest that around 70 million people died owing to the constant battles that were fought between 1939 and 1945. Around two-thirds of this figure actually comprised civilians who had not engaged in war, which made it the deadliest war in history. Close to one in 10 Germans perished during the war. Germany lost around 30 per cent of its total armed personnel. More than 15 million Chinese died during World War II, while the Soviet Union saw casualties of around 27 million. Poland lost 16 per cent of its population, mainly Jews who were exterminated as per Hitler's final solution plan. In a nutshell, World War II witnessed killings of around 30,000 people every day.

American military truck in Pilsen City Czech Republic Europe - Anniversary at the end of World War II.

Soldiers on a farmhouse after World War II.

World War II Memorial in Washington DC.